WORDS

BILL LARREMORE

Copyright © 2021 Bill Larremore
ISBN Print: 978-0-578-98287-8
ISBN Ebook: 978-0-578-98288-5
All rights reserved.

Contents

Preface i

CHAPTER I: God's Words 1

CHAPTER II: Decree a Thing! 7

CHAPTER III: Trust in the Lord 17

CHAPTER IV: Confessing and Believing 23
1. We are forgiven 26
2. We are saved 28
3. We are the seed of Abraham 29
4. We are the righteousness of God, and He increases the harvest of our righteousness 31
5. We have been moved to a place of abundance 32
6. We are very wealthy 33
7. We walk in divine prosperity 35
8. We have a blood covenant with God 37
9. Our youth is renewed like the eagle 39
10. God trains our hands for war, and our fingers for battle 40
11. We walk in divine health 41
12. We are full of wisdom and understanding 44
13. We have great faith 46
14. We are blessed and highly favored 48
15. Angels watch over us 52

CHAPTER V: Have a Vision 55

CHAPTER VI: Conclusion 61

About the Author 69

Preface

God has been talking to me, in my spirit, for quite some time about writing a small book that will help Christians and non-Christians understand how powerful their words can be. I have been reluctant because I was not sure I was hearing from God, but He has been persistent. I want to be an obedient believer and a doer of God's word. I was raised in the church, and studied God's word haphazardly for years. Then came 5 years in the military, and I seemed to have forgotten all that I had learned about God. I had close friends that liked to drink all the time, and I kept telling myself that I enjoyed it and their friendship, but I was missing out on life, and lost my first wife through a divorce.

I decided that I had to make a commitment to God, myself, and the people around me that I cared about before they were no longer part of my life. I did not want to lose them, so I committed to making a change. I had been very lax about studying and reading the word of God for quite a few years. I thought about what type of legacy I would be leaving my family. What would my wife and kids say about me when I got older? I was being very slack, for use of a better word, about learning and studying God's word. What God has said in His Word about being with my family, and implementing that word into my life has been foremost; especially for me, these last few years. I still have a way to go, but I am trying and committed to God, my wife, our kids, and the vision and assignment God has given to me to fulfill. Some of the things God has shown me, I could not have believed several years ago. I am still learning.

Words are particularly important and powerful. I have seen words tear down a person's self-esteem, and I have seen words build a person's self-esteem up and renew their self-worth. It is my desire that by you reading this book, your life will be changed, and you will learn and understand the power of what you are saying with their words. Also, what we say about our lives, our family, our job, and the way we see ourselves is also especially important. Proverbs 18 states "**Death and life are in the power of the tongue** " You are a King in this life. Royalty. Learn to live like a King, and speak or decree things like you are a King.

CHAPTER I

God's Words

CHAPTER I

God's Words

Words are of great importance; it is how we communicate. Everything that we say carries power and authority. We express our feelings with words. Words bring peace, or words can start a war. Compassion is expressed by the way we speak to each other. Love and hate can be distinguished with the words we use. God used His words to create all that is, from the dust on the ground to the stars in the universe. God put His spirit in us, and expected us to be like Him. We are made in His image.

Genesis 1: 26 New American Standard Bible (NASB) "Then God said, "Let Us make mankind **in Our image**, according to **Our** likeness; and let them rule over the fish of the sea and over the birds of the sky and over the livestock and over all the earth, and over every crawling thing that crawls on the earth."

Hebrews 11:3 (NASB) "³ By faith we understand that the worlds were prepared by the **Word** of God, so that what is seen was not made out of things which are visible."

I am somewhat of a textualist and believe that the Bible was written for every one of us. What the Bible says, I take somewhat literally. If the Bible says that I am forgiven, then I find scriptures that tell me I have been forgiven. If the Bible tells me that I am healed of every sickness or disease, then I find scriptures that tell me that Jesus has healed me of all my infirmities. If the Bible tells me that I am rich, I find the scriptures that say I am rich. I do not just read those scriptures one or two times. I meditate on the verses and read them many times until it is in my heart, and I know that what I am saying is real.

Let me say here that whatever the Bible says, that is the way I pray. I use God's word.

Mathew 18:8-9 New Kings James Version (NKJV) "⁸ If your hand or foot causes you to sin, cut it off and cast *it* from you. It is better for you to enter into life lame or maimed, rather than having two hands or two feet, to be cast into the everlasting fire. ⁹ And if your eye causes you to sin, pluck it out and cast *it* from you. It is better for you to enter into life with one eye, rather than having two eyes, to be cast into hell fire."

You are not to pluck your eye out, or cut a limb off. Many times, you must read the whole chapter to understand what is being said, and to receive the full meaning. You are never to mutilate your body because it is the temple of God.

Sometimes I will use various versions of the Bible until I understand what God is telling me. I may not feel like I am forgiven, healed, or rich, but God inspired the writing of the

Bible, God and His word cannot lie. There are thousands of promises that God has given to each of us, so we do not have to live in a barely get by world working 2 or 3 jobs, sick, broke, and depressed.

There are a lot of people and preachers, I am sad to say, that will try to help us misunderstand what is written in the Bible by saying that it was written for the people that lived back in that day. The Bible has no power in today's world.

Why is only part of God's word relevant today, and not all of it. Most believe that Salvation is for today. It is a free gift from God. Health is for today; it is a free gift from God. I have been healed of back trouble. Prosperity is for today; it is a free gift from God. God provided for me and my family when I was laid off on several occasions. Once for over 2 years, and another for a year. We always had food on the table, and all of our bills were paid, including our utilities. The utilities were never shut off. In turn, there are also a lot of people and preachers that live by God's word, and live a life of abundance, and health by doing and confessing what they have found to be their promises. I can say that I am one of them, and I have been blessed so tremendously.

Words have power. God demonstrated this in Genesis 1: 3 NASB. "³ Then God **said**, "Let there be light"; and there was light. " Throughout the first chapter of Genesis "God **said**" and it came to pass. Words were used by God to create rather than to communicate, and we were created in His image and likeness.

In Proverbs 18:21 NASB God told us that "Death and life are in **the power of the tongue**, And those who love it will eat its fruit."

Some negative examples of this, although the words may sound harmless: My feet are KILLING me. You are making me NUTS. You are driving me CRAZY. I am just DIEING to go. You make me SICK. Will you never LEARN. Are you that STUPID? You just SLAY me.

Also, on the other hand, never say to your kids; You will never amount to anything. You are so clumsy. How stupid is that. What were you thinking? What is wrong with your memory. Ask God to forgive you and start speaking Blessings over them. Tell your kids that they are very smart, very handsome (pretty), and destined for great things. Tell them they have a blessed memory. Do not destroy your children's self-esteem with negative words. Your children will remember the negative things said about them, and then repeat those things until they believe them. Build them up with words of encouragement.

Proverbs 22:6 NASB "⁶ Train up a child in the way he should go, Even when he grows older he will not abandon it."

I think the way The Living Bible says it the best.

Proverbs 22:6 The Living Bible (TLB) "⁶ Teach a child to choose the right path, and when he is older, he will remain upon it."

CHAPTER II

Decree a Thing!

CHAPTER II

Decree a Thing!

I have a confession that I read over me and my family every day because I believe in the power of my words. Every word can be found in His scriptures. I got this confession from several pastors I heard on TV. I combined them because the words are so powerful and have changed my way of living, thinking, and speaking. This confession is on my home computer, my work computer, in my briefcase, and on our refrigerator. This way is it always before me, even if I am out of town, I take a copy with me.

"In the name of Jesus, I decree from this moment forward that I see myself the way God sees me, as highly Blessed, needing and wanting nothing. I am highly Favored of the Lord. I am receiving and in the Blessing explosion. I am crowned with Glory and Honor. I am the Righteousness of God in Christ Jesus. I am reigning as a king in life through the one-man Jesus Christ the Messiah. Now in Jesus name, I declare by Faith that

I walk in divine Favor. I have preferential treatment, supernatural increase. I have restoration, I have prominence, I have petitions granted, laws changed, policies and rules changed, and battles won which I do not have to fight. Why? All because of Favor, the Blessing and Favor of God is on my life in Jesus name. Every morning when I arise, I will speak and expect Divine Favor to go before me and surround me as with a shield, with good will and pleasures for evermore. Rules and laws are changed because of the favor of God. My youth is renewed like the eagle; my vitality is restored, I am full of sap and very green, and forget none of your benefits since I am the seed of Abraham. The Favor of God causes my family and I to walk in divine and uncommon Health, Prosperity, Abundances, and Protection. Doors are now opened for me that men have said are impossible to open. No obstacle can stop me; no hindrance can delay me in Jesus name. Because of the Favor of God, I will thrive, increase, enlarge my territory, grow, prosper, abound, spread out, expand, make steady progress, be at a high point in my life, have an exceptionally long and full life, and my memory is Blessed of the Lord. All our children will be taught of and by the LORD, and great will be their peace. This is my season for flourishing. I am a living memorial to show that the Lord is Faithful to His promises. As Abraham, I am very rich in cattle, silver, and gold. I am marked to be Blessed, and envied. The Blessing of God on my life empowers me to prosper, and the Favor of God produces the opportunity. I am honored by my Father as I receive genuine Favor that comes directly from God. I am special to Him, I am the object of His affection, I am the apple of His eye, I am Blessed and highly Favored of the Lord in Jesus name. Father, I ask that you show me your Glory, and avenge me of my adversaries, and I thank You for my recompence. Amen and so be it right now in Jesus name. Thank you, Lord, it is done in the name of Jesus."

The reason that I start with "I decree" is because once you have made Jesus the Lord over your life, I have been set up to be a king in life that rules and reigns with Jesus who sits at the right hand of God the Father. Jesus is the Head, and we are his body.

In Micah 4:9 NASB states "⁹ Is there no king among you,".

The answer is YES. You are a king through Jesus. You are an heir and joint heir with Jesus when you ask Him into your heart. Jesus sits at the right hand of the Father.

Job 22:28 NASB "You will also decree a thing, and it will be established for you;".

Proverbs 16:10 NASB "¹⁰ the lips of the king; His mouth should not err in judgment."

Romans 5:17 Amplified Bible, Classic Edition (AMPC) "¹⁷ For if because of one man's trespass (lapse, offense) death **reign**ed through that one, much more surely will those who receive [God's] overflowing grace (unmerited favor) and the free gift of righteousness [putting them into right standing **with** Himself] **reign** as kings in life through the one Man Jesus **Christ** (the Messiah, the Anointed One)."

Also, Romans 5:21 AMPC "²¹ So that, [just] as sin has

reigned in death, [so] grace (His unearned and undeserved favor) might **reign** also through righteousness (right standing **with** God) which issues in eternal life through Jesus **Christ** (the Messiah, the Anointed One) our Lord."

If you have never made Jesus Christ the Lord of your life, it is a free gift from God. Simply say, "Father, I believe that Jesus died for me and rose again taking all my sins, and I ask that you forgive me, make me a new creature, and come into my heart".

That is all that is required to be saved and forgiven. You are now a child of the King of Kings and an heir to all the promises of God. Now find a church home that will teach you what Gods' word says, and a good Bible believing church will help you strengthen your growing faith.

John 3:16-17 NASB "[16] For God so loved the world, that He gave His only begotten Son, that whoever believes in Him shall not perish, but have eternal life. [17] For God did not send the Son into the world to judge the world, but that the world might be saved through Him.",

And Romans 10:9-10 NASB "[9] that if you confess with your mouth Jesus *as* Lord, and believe in your heart that God raised Him from the dead, you will be saved; [10] for with the heart a person believes, resulting in righteousness, and with the mouth he confesses, resulting in salvation."

Romans 10:9-10 AMPC " [9] Because if you acknowledge *and* confess with your lips that Jesus is Lord and in your heart believe (adhere to, trust in, and rely on the truth) that God raised Him from the dead, you will be saved. [10] For with the heart a person believes (adheres to, trusts in, and relies on Christ) and so is justified (declared righteous, acceptable to God), and with the mouth he confesses (declares openly and speaks out freely his faith) *and* confirms [his] salvation."

I Corinthians 2:9-12 NASB "9 but just as it is written: Things which eye has not seen and ear has not heard, and which have not entered the human heart, all that God has prepared for those who love Him. 10 For to us God revealed *them* through the Spirit; for the Spirit searches all things, even the depths of God. 11 For who among people knows the *thoughts* of a person except the spirit of the person that is in him? So also, the *thoughts* of God no one knows, except the Spirit of God. 12 Now we have not received the spirit of the world, but the Spirit who is from God, so that we may know the things freely given to us by God."

II Corinthians 5:17 NASB "17 Therefore, if any man is in Christ, he is a new creature. The old things passed away: behold new things have come."

II Corinthians 5:17 Kings James Version (KJV) "17 Therefore, if any man is in Christ, he is a new creature. Old things have passed away. Look, all things have become new."

You now have a new life, your sins are forgiven, and your past has been removed in the sight of God. It does not matter what you may have done in your past, it is wiped clean in the sight of God. He will not remember your past, and neither should you.

Now that you have made Jesus the Lord of your life, you

have the same Faith that Jesus had, and the same rights and privileges to use His Name. He used words to accomplish all that He did on this earth. In Romans 12:3 NASB he states, "For through the grace given to me I say to everyone among you not to think more highly **of** himself than he ought to think; but to think so as to have sound judgment, as God has allotted to each a **measure of faith**."

We must use and develop our measure of Faith so that our Faith will grow in us.

In John 14:12 NASB Jesus says "[12] Truly, truly, I say to you, he who believes in Me, the works that I do, he will do also; and greater *works* than these he will do; because I go to the Father."

Jesus used his Faith, by setting the example, to accomplish all that is written about his life, and we are to do what He did. Even greater things.

The following are various translations of Hebrews 11:1. Each say the same thing, but the wording is somewhat different. By reading various translations, I sometimes get a better perspective or understanding of what God is telling me in His Word.

Hebrews 11:1 NASB "Now faith is the assurance of *things* hoped for, the conviction of things not seen."

Hebrews 11:1 KJV "Now faith is the substance of things hoped for, the evidence of things not seen."

Hebrews 11:1 The Message Bible (MSG) "The fundamental

fact of existence is that this trust in God, this faith, is the firm foundation under everything that makes life worth living."

Hebrews 11:1 AMPC "Now faith is the assurance (the confirmation, the title deed) of the things [we] hope for, being the proof of things [we] do not see *and* the conviction of their reality [faith perceiving as real fact what is not revealed to the senses]."

Hebrews 11:1 Contemporary English Version (CEV) "Faith makes us sure of what we hope for and gives us proof of what we cannot see."

I urge you to start now in believing for something that is impossible for you. It might be healing of your body, a new suit, a new pair of shoes, a better car, a better job, or a better place to live. You have to start somewhere, so your Faith will grow and mature. We have the same measure of Faith that Jesus had. Now let us grow and develop that Faith.

Like I said, there are thousands of promises in the Bible. Find those that apply to your situation or need and start confessing and believing that you have what God has promised you. It is part of your inheritance.

Take for instant the woman in Mathew 9:20-22 AMPC "[20] And behold, a woman who had suffered from a flow of blood for twelve years came up behind Him and touched the fringe of His garment;[21] **For she kept saying to herself**, If I only touch His garment, I shall be restored to health.[22] Jesus turned around and, seeing her, He said, Take courage, daughter! Your **faith** has made you well. And at once the woman was restored to health."

Words

As it said in the Amplified, "For she kept saying to herself". Continue to think about what God has said to you through His word, the Bible. This is meditation and it will build your faith to received what God has promised you. Keep saying. Cut out some of the TV you may be watching, or get up a little ea rlier, but make time for God and He will make time for you.

CHAPTER III

Trust in the Lord

CHAPTER III

Trust in the Lord

Whatever you are believing for the Lord to give you or bring you through, you have to Trust in God that He will give you the desires of your heart. Do not waver in your believing.

Psalm 37:4-5 NASB "⁴ Delight yourself in the Lord; And He will give you the desires of your heart. ⁵ Commit your way to the Lord, Trust also in Him, and He will do it."

John 16:23-24 NASB "²³ In that day you will not question Me about anything. Truly, truly, I say to you, if you ask the Father for anything in My name, He will give it to you. ²⁴ Until now you have asked for nothing in My name; ask and you will receive, so that your joy may be made full. "

John 16:23-24 MSG " ²³⁻²⁴ "This is what I want you to do: Ask the Father for whatever is in keeping with the things I've revealed to you. Ask in my name, according to my will, and he'll most certainly give it to you. Your joy will be a river overflowing its banks!"

John 16:23-24 AMPC "And when that time comes, you will ask nothing of Me [you will need to ask Me no questions]. I assure you, most solemnly I tell you, that My Father will grant you whatever you ask in My Name [as presenting all that I Am]. ²⁴ Up to this time you have not asked a [single] thing in My Name [as presenting all that I Am]; but now ask *and* **keep on asking** and you will receive, so that your joy (gladness, delight) may be full *and* complete."

God wants and desires you to be happy and full of joy. He has made it so amazingly easy for us. It is a free gift that you do not have to work for. There is nothing that you can do to earn this free gift except to receive it in Jesus Name. He said in Psalm 149:4 NASB "⁴ For the Lord takes pleasure in His people; He will beautify the afflicted ones with salvation."

God wants you to have all that He has promised you. Use your Faith and receive. It is that simple. He never ask you to pay or work for anything. Only believe.

John 15:7 NASB ". ⁷ If you abide in Me, and My words abide in you, ask **whatever you wish**, and it will be done for you."

John 15:11 NASB "¹¹ These things I have spoken to you so that My joy may be in you, and *that* your joy may be made full."

You are to be like a small child jumping into a swimming pool trusting that your dad will catch you. You know that your dad will catch you and not let you sink. A child just trust that nothing will go wrong when he jumps in the pool because daddy will always catch him. God is our daddy. We are to be just like a small child, and trust God completely to always be there for us, and to always be true to his word. God will not lie to us. What God has said, God will do. Not only for you but for me also.

I want my joy to be made full and complete, and I want to be happy with myself knowing that I have done all that God has ask me to do. What will make your joy complete? Write down what you think will make your joy complete. You could be wanting a family, a new house, or a new car. It could be that you want to start a new business, or just a chance to retire from your job earlier than you have planned. It does not matter what you desire, just make sure that the desire lines up with what God is telling you to do. He has such a great plan for you and your family. He did say in Ephesians:

Ephesians 3:20 NASB "[20] Now to Him who is able to do far more abundantly beyond all that we ask or think, according to the power that works within us."

Ask God to give you a vision of where He wants to take you, and what He wants you to do. Ask God for wisdom and understanding, and to show you what will truly make you happy and fulfilled. Think about that. Meditate on God's word in regard to you. Ask God to help you find scriptures that will allow you to dream for bigger and better things, and develop and stretch your faith for those things. Believe God to fulfill His word in your life, but above all; Trust in God and what His word says about you, and He will make your joy complete.

When I was looking for a wife over 30+ years ago, I was specific, and ask God for a beautiful, loving, affectionate, caring, virtuous woman who loved God as much as I do. A Proverbs 31 women. I received exactly what I prayed and ask for, and have been incredibly happy with the woman that God gave me.

The following are the confessions that I have made, or I am making, and believing because God said so.

CHAPTER IV

Confessing and Believing

CHAPTER IV

Confessing and Believing

This chapter consist of the things that I am confessing and believing for me and my family. I have listed some scriptures to back up my confession, but there are many, many more that I have not listed here. Some of my desires have already come to pass. Some things I am still believing for, but I know that we have already received them according to:

Mark 11:22-24 NASB "²² And Jesus answered saying to them, "Have faith in God. ²³ Truly I say to you, whoever says to this mountain, 'Be taken up and cast into the sea,' and does not doubt in his heart, but believes that what he says is going to happen, it will be *granted* him. ²⁴ Therefore I say to you, all things for which you pray and ask, believe that you have received them, and they will be *granted* you".

You may use the scriptures below or find the promises that apply to you, or I encourage you to find the promises that relate to what you desire to come into your life. Be specific. For an example: Don't just say, "I just want a husband/wife". Well, that may be exactly what you get, and you may not be happy with what you get; just any old husband/wife. Instead pray for exactly what you desire in a husband/wife. Do not settle for any old…. Always be specific in what you pray for and desire.

1. We are forgiven

It does not matter what we have done. God will forgive us if we ask Him. He said that He will cast all our sins into the Sea of Forgetfulness, and remembers them no more. Many things I have to ask for forgiveness several times.

Romans 10:10 AMPC "[10] For with the heart a person believes (adheres to, trusts in, and relies on Christ) and so is justified (declared righteous, acceptable to God), and with the mouth he confesses (declares openly and speaks out freely his faith) *and* confirms [his] salvation."

When I do anything wrong, I am quick to ask God to forgive me "In the name of Jesus", and He is quick to forgive me when I repent. If I speak badly about anyone, I ask God to forgive me. Even if I think bad thoughts about someone, I ask God to forgive me. I do not want any hinderance to come between me and God. That is the only way I can be forgiven and blessed by God.

Jesus talks about a man's heart, and the things that are in our heart comes out when we speak. It can be bitterness, hate, or wisdom, love, and compassion. It is also very important to forgive all those who have wronged you, or who you disagree with. I have quit watching the news on TV because I would get angry with the other political party. I have learned to forgive them and pray God's mercy, wisdom, and understanding for them..

Mathew 12:35-37 NKJV "[35] A good man out of the good treasure of his heart brings forth good things, and an evil man out of the evil treasure brings forth evil things. [36] But I say to you that for every idle word men may speak; they will give account of it in the day of judgment. [37] For by your words you will be justified, and by your words you will be condemned."

Mark 11:22-26 NASB "[22] And Jesus answered saying to them, "Have faith in God. [23] Truly I say to you, whoever says to this mountain, 'Be taken up and cast into the sea,' and does not doubt in his heart, but believes that what he says is going to happen, it will be *granted* him. [24] Therefore I say to you, all things for which you pray and ask, believe that you have received them, and they will be *granted* you. [25] Whenever you stand praying, forgive, if you have anything against anyone, so that your Father who is in heaven will also forgive you your transgressions. [26] But if you do not forgive, neither will your Father who is in heaven forgive your transgressions."

As you can see, words are immensely powerful. They can tear you down or build you up. We must always watch what we say, but saying is not enough. You must add Faith to your words, and forgive those that have hurt us. It does not matter what they have done, forgive them so God can forgive you.

Unforgiveness is a hinderance and a block in receiving any gift from God as God has said in:

Mark 11:25-26 NASB "[25] Whenever you stand praying, forgive, if you have anything against anyone, so that your Father who is in heaven will also forgive you your transgressions. [26] But if you do not forgive, neither will your Father who is in heaven forgive your transgressions."

As you can see it does not matter what they have done, forgive them so God can forgive you. Unforgiveness is a hinderance and will block you from receiving any gift from God.

Always use His words in your prayers and request. The angels only listen to Gods word. Speak God's word when you pray.

Psalm 103:20 KJV "[20] Bless the Lord, ye his angels, that **excel in strength**, that do his commandments, hearkening unto the voice of his word."

It is very important that when you pray, you pray God's word. Use his words even when talking to friends. Be ever mindful of our Fathers words. It pleases God when we use the words He has written.

2. We are saved

Once we have ask Jesus into our heart, God is faithful and true to His word to come into our hearts, and make us a new person.

John 3:16 NASB "[16] For God so loved the world, that He

gave His only begotten Son, that whoever believes in Him shall not perish, but have eternal life."

Romans 10:8-10 NASB "⁸ But what does it say? "The word is near you, in your mouth and in your heart" (that is, the word of faith which we preach): ⁹ that if you confess with your mouth the Lord Jesus and believe in your heart that God has raised Him from the dead, you will be saved. ¹⁰ For with the heart one believes unto righteousness, and with the mouth confession is made unto salvation."

I have asked Jesus to come into my heart, and He came in, and made me a new person. If you have asked Jesus into your heart, you are also saved, sanctified, and made the righteousness of God through his son Jesus. All that is required is for you to ask.

3. We are the seed of Abraham

When we ask Jesus into our heart, we become part of the family of God, and become an heir of Abraham.

Genesis 13:1-3 NASB "Now the LORD had said to Abram: "Get out of your country, From your family And from your father's house To a land that I will show you. ² I will make you a great nation; I will bless you And make your name great; And you shall be a blessing. ³ I will bless those who bless you, And I will curse him who curses you; And in you all the families of the earth shall be blessed."

Genesis 13:2 NASB "² Abram had become very wealthy in livestock and in silver and gold."

Genesis 22:18 NASB "¹⁸ In **your seed** all the nations of the earth shall be blessed, because you have obeyed My voice."

Galatians 3:29 NASB "²⁹ And if you belong to Christ, then you are Abraham's descendants, heirs according to promise."

When I ask Jesus to come into my heart, I then became a descendant of Abraham, and intitled to the provisions and promises that God made to Abraham, and my inheritance as an heir according to the promise. God has given me His word through a blood covenant which he made with Abraham. I do not take that covenant lightly, and God always honors His word to us in that covenant if we will let Him. By not trusting God, we tie His hands to do for us the things He said He would do. We are an heir through Jesus our savior.

Websters 1828 dictionary defines an Heir as: **HEIR**, *noun* are. [Latin haeres, haeredis.]

1. The man who succeeds, or is to succeed another in the possession of lands, tenements, and hereditaments, by descent; the man on whom the law casts an estate of inheritance by the death of the ancestor or former possessor; or the man in whom the title to an estate of inheritance is vested by the operation of law, on the death of a former owner.

We give the title to a person who is to inherit after the death of an ancestor, and during his life, as well as to the person who has actually come into possession. A man's children are his heirs. In most monarchies, the king's eldest son is *heir* to the throne; and a nobleman's eldest son is *heir* to his title.

Lo, one born in my house is my *heir* Genesis 15:3.

4. One who is entitled to possess. In Scripture, saints are called heirs of the promise, heirs of righteousness, heirs of salvation, etc., by virtue of the death of Christ, or of God's gracious promises.

4. We are the righteousness of God, and He increases the harvest of our righteousness

It is God that makes righteous. There is nothing that we can do go get righteous. It all comes from God. As we give to the ministry, as God directs, our righteousness is increased.

II Corinthians 5:20-22 AMPC "[20] Therefore, we are ambassadors for Christ, as though God were making an appeal through us; we beg you on behalf of Christ, be reconciled to God. [21] He made Him who knew no sin *to be* sin on our behalf, so that we might become the righteousness of God in Him."

II Corinthians 9:10 NASB "[10] Now He who supplies seed to the sower and bread for food will supply and multiply your seed for sowing and increase the harvest of your righteousness."

You have to see yourself as God sees you. When you ask God for forgiveness in Jesus's name, He makes you righteous in His sight. As you partner or support ministries financially, God also increases the harvest of your righteousness. Righteousness along with faith is a shield that cannot be penetrated by any demonic forces.

5. We have been moved to a place of abundance

We are not to be living in lack, not enough, or just get by. It is God's plan for us to have more than enough.

Psalms 37:11 NASB "[11] But the humble will inherit the land And will delight themselves in abundant prosperity."

Psalm 66:12 NASB "[12] ...Yet You brought us out into *a place of* abundance."

And John 10:10 NASB "[10] The thief comes only to steal and kill and destroy; I came that they may have life, and have *it* abundantly."

Malachi 3:10-12 NASB "[10] Bring the whole tithe into the storehouse, so that there may be food in My house, and test Me now in this," says the LORD of hosts, "if I will not open for you the windows of heaven and pour out for you **a blessing until it overflows**. [11] Then I will rebuke the devourer for you, so that it will not destroy the fruits of the ground; nor will your vine in the field cast *its grapes*," says the LORD of hosts. [12] "All the nations will call you blessed, for you shall be a delightful land," says the LORD of hosts."

I want an overflowing blessing in every area of my life. God said that He would give it to us IF we obeyed him and not rob Him of our tithes. To have an abundance is better than just getting by from paycheck to paycheck. Or if there is more month than money. It is nice to take your family out to eat or go on vacation together, and not worry about what the financial cost will be. Or to see someone that is in need of something, and be able to take care of that need, whether it be a pair of shoes, a meal, or a house payment. Maybe it is to purchase a car or house for someone. To have that kind of overflowing blessing, as told to us by God in Malachi, is wonderful. I believe that God will give you the things that you have ask for, or the thing to get the things. It is part of the overflowing blessing.

6. We are very wealthy

God wants and needs us to be wealthy. There is so much that can be done in the service of God, and finances are needed to do that. He has made us to be His distribution centers to progress His kingdom.

Deuteronomy 8:18 NASB "¹⁸ But you shall remember the LORD your God, for it is He who is giving you power to make wealth, that He may confirm His covenant which He swore to your fathers, as *it is* this day."

Deuteronomy 29:9 KJV "⁹ Keep therefore the words of this covenant, and do them, that ye may prosper in all that ye do."

Psalm 35:27 KJV "²⁷ Let them shout for joy and rejoice, who favor my vindication; And let them say continually, "The LORD be magnified, Who delights in the prosperity of His servant.""

Psalm 112:3 NASB "³ Wealth and riches are in his house, And his righteousness endures forever."

Psalm 118:25 NASB "²⁵ O Lord, do save, we beseech You; O Lord, we beseech You, do send prosperity!"

Proverbs 8:21 NASB "²¹ To endow those who love me with wealth, That I may fill their treasuries."

Proverbs 10:4-6 KJV "⁴ He becometh poor that dealeth with a slack hand: but the hand of the diligent maketh rich. ⁵ He that gathereth in summer is a wise son: but he that sleepeth in harvest is a son that causeth shame. ⁶ Blessings are upon the head of the just:"

Proverbs 10:22 KJV "²² The blessing of the Lord, it maketh rich, and he addeth no sorrow with it."

I Corinthians 2:9 AMPC "⁹ But, on the contrary, as the Scripture says, What eye has not seen and ear has not heard and has not entered into the heart of man, [all that] God has prepared (made and keeps ready) for those who love Him [who hold Him in affectionate reverence, promptly obeying Him and gratefully recognizing the benefits He has bestowed]."

Ephesians 3:20 NASB "²⁰ Now to Him who is able to do far more abundantly beyond all that we ask or think, according to the power that works within us."

This is not to be considered greed. God is an extravagant God. Jesus's first miracle was to turn water into wine. It was excellent wine according to the wine taster at the wedding. He wants you to have the absolute best in everything.

Like He said in Ephesians 3:20 NASB "²⁰ Now to Him

who is able to do far more abundantly beyond all that we **ask or think**, according to the power that works within us."

God wants and needs us to be wealthy. There is so much that can be done in the service of God, and finances are needed to do that. If your pastor is in need of a new car, would it be nice if you could tell him to go get whatever car he wants, and send the bill to you. Expanding any ministry needs finances, and I believe that Christians are to be wealthy in order to finance the expansion of His kingdom. God is ready to bestow on each of us the things that He has made ready for us. It is not to show off and say with a prideful spirit, "Look what I have", but to say, "Look what the Lord has done for me". Sow a seed above your tithe, and watch how the Lord multiplies it.

7. We walk in divine prosperity

God provides all that we need. All we have to do is ask Him for it, and believe that we receive it. He will make a way. Abundance, wealth, and prosperity may sound like the same thing, but each are a different gift of God.

Deuteronomy 1:11 KJV "[11] May the LORD, the God of your fathers, increase you a thousand-fold more than you are and bless you, just as He has promised you!"

Deuteronomy 6:10:11 NASB "[10] Then it shall come about when the LORD your God brings you into the land which He swore to your fathers, Abraham, Isaac and Jacob, to give you, great and splendid cities which you did not build, [11] and houses full of all good things which you did not fill, and hewn cisterns which you did not dig, vineyards and olive trees which you did not plant."

Deuteronomy 28:2-8 NASB "² All these blessings will come upon you and overtake you if you obey the LORD your God: ³ "Blessed *shall* you *be* in the city, and blessed *shall* you *be* in the country." ⁴ "Blessed *shall be* the offspring of your body and the produce of your ground and the offspring of your beasts, the increase of your herd and the young of your flock." ⁵ "Blessed *shall be* your basket and your kneading bowl." ⁶ "Blessed *shall* you *be* when you come in, and blessed *shall* you *be* when you go out." ⁷ "The LORD shall cause your enemies who rise up against you to be defeated before you; they will come out against you one way and will flee before you seven ways." ⁸ The LORD will command the blessing upon you in your barns and in all that you put your hand to, and He will bless you in the land which the LORD your God gives you."

Proverbs 3:9-10 KJV "⁹ Honor the LORD from your wealth And from the first of all your produce; ¹⁰ So your barns will be filled with plenty, And your vats will overflow with new wine."

II Corinthians 9:8 NASB "⁸ And God is able to make all grace abound to you, so that always having all sufficiency in everything, you may have an abundance for every good deed;"

This goes along with being moved to a place of abundance,

and being very wealthy. Prosperity is not just finances, but life itself. It is to receive a promotion when no one else is being promoted, or getting a raise when no one else is getting a raise. Gods Prosperity will meet all your needs. To meet any need that comes along whether it is your need or someone else's' need is a wonderful thing. All throughout God's word, He talks about taking care of His children, and giving them everything that is needed. God is a generous God. Because He loves you and me, He is wanting to give His children all that they desire. It is just like us to want to give our children all that they desire.

Romans 8:37-39 NASB "[37] But in all these things we overwhelmingly conquer through Him who loved us. [38] For I am convinced that neither death, nor life, nor angels, nor principalities, nor things present, nor things to come, nor powers, [39] nor height, nor depth, nor any other created thing, will be able to separate us from the love of God, which is in Christ Jesus our Lord."

God genuinely loves you and me, and will go to any length to give us our desires.

8. We have a blood covenant with God

When we ask Jesus into our hearts, God also seals it with a blood covenant. People in the west have a difficult time understanding how strong a blood covenant is. It means that what is yours is His, and what is His is yours. God will fight for you because you are one of His now.

Galatians 4:7 NASB "⁷ Therefore you are no longer a slave, but a son; and if a son, then an heir through God."

Acts 3:25 NASB "It is you who are the sons of the prophets and of the **covenant** which **God** made **with** your fathers, saying to Abraham, 'And in your seed all the families of the earth shall be blessed.'"

Galatians 3:29 NASB "²⁹ And if you belong to Christ, then you are Abraham's descendants, heirs according to promise."

Romans 8:31-39 (MSG) "³¹⁻³⁹ So, what do you think? With God on our side like this, how can we lose? If God did not hesitate to put everything on the line for us, embracing our condition and exposing himself to the worst by sending his own Son, is there anything else he wouldn't gladly and freely do for us? And who would dare tangle with God by messing with one of God's chosen? Who would dare even to point a finger? The One who died for us—who was raised to life for us!—is in the presence of God at this very moment sticking up for us. Do you think anyone is going to be able to drive a wedge between us and Christ's love for us? There is no way! Not trouble, not hard times, not hatred, not hunger, not homelessness, not bullying threats, not backstabbing, not even the worst sins listed in Scripture: They kill us in cold blood because they hate you. We are sitting ducks; they pick us off one by one. None of this fazes us because Jesus loves us. I'm absolutely convinced that nothing—nothing living or dead, angelic or demonic, today or tomorrow, high or low, thinkable or unthinkable—absolutely *nothing* can get between us and God's love because of the way that Jesus our Master has embraced us."

God has made a Blood Covenant with those that have accepted Jesus as their Lord through Abraham because He loves us so much.. That intitles us to everything that God has. God is not poor. His streets are paved with gold. He has given each one of us a mansion in Heaven. But here on earth, He said that he would fight for us and take care of us. A Covenant of this type means that whatever God has in Heaven and on earth, we are to take part in and have it also. We are His children.

9. Our youth is renewed like the eagle

It has always been the quest for the fountain of youth. God has provided that fountain in His Word. My wife and I started praying that our youth would be renewed like the eagle years ago, and no one knows that we are 20+ years older than we are.

Psalms 92:14-15 NASB "[14] They will still yield fruit in old age; They shall be full of sap and very green, [15] To declare that the LORD is upright; *He is* my rock, and there is no unrighteousness in Him."

Psalms 103:5 NASB "Who satisfies your years with good things, *So that* your youth is renewed like the eagle."

People have been looking for the spring that will restore their youth since Cortez said he found it. There are even research to discover the chromosome that causes aging.

Having your youth being restored, and feeling or looking young is what people have been searching for, for hundreds of years.

This is just one of the gifts of God. Moses was still climbing mountains when he was 120 years old. Caleb was fighting and winning battles when he was in his 80's. That is the way I want to go out, strong in my body and mind. That is the way you should want to live. Long and strong.

10. God trains our hands for war, and our fingers for battle

There may come a time when we will have to fight for what we believe (spiritually and physically), and for our families. Caleb was in his 80's when he fought for the land God had promised him.

Psalms 18:34 NASB "[34] He trains my hands for battle, So that my arms can bend a bow of bronze."

Psalms 144:1 NASB "[1] Blessed be the LORD, my rock, Who trains my hands for war, *And* my fingers for battle;"

Ephesians 6:10-13 NASB "[10] Finally, be strong in the Lord and in the strength of His might. [11] Put on the full armor of God, so that you will be able to stand firm against the schemes of the devil. [12] For our struggle is not against flesh and blood, but against the rulers, against the powers, against the world forces of this darkness, against the spiritual *forces* of wickedness in the heavenly *places*. [13] Therefore, take up the full armor of God, so that you will be able to resist in the evil day, and having done everything, to stand firm."

Abram, or Abraham, took 318 men from his household, and destroyed three kings and their armies because they had his nephew Lot and his family. God gave him the strategy to win in battle. But we also have to fight everyday against the devil. The devil is constantly trying to take over our minds by putting thoughts in our mind that will get us hurt, ruin our family relationships, or even get us killed. That is his job, to steal, kill and destroy. He has no respect for any human, and is doing all that he can to destroy us. That is why we must constantly seek God's will and wisdom, and God's way of doing things. We are more than conquerors as in Romans 8:37 AMPC "37 Yet amid all these things we are **more than conquerors** *and* gain a surpassing victory through Him Who loved us."

11. We walk in divine health

It is no fun being sick, or having a disease that is debilitating, nor incurable. God created us, and said that He is our health and strength. How can we be a witness for Him and His mercy if we are sick? His desire for us is to be in full health. Jesus healed and restored all that came to Him, and He is still healing and restoring all those who ask Him.

Psalms 107:20 CEV "20 By the power of his own word, he healed you and saved you from destruction."

Isaiah 53:5 NASB "5 But He was pierced through for our transgressions, He was crushed for our iniquities; The chastening for our well-being *fell* upon Him, And by His scourging we are healed."

Jeremiah 30:17 NASB "³⁰ For I will restore you to health And I will heal you of your wounds,' declares the LORD,"

Mathew 4:23 NASB "²³ Jesus was going throughout all Galilee, teaching in their synagogues and proclaiming the gospel of the kingdom, and healing every kind of disease and every kind of sickness among the people."

Mathew 8:17 NASB "¹⁷ *This was* to fulfill what was spoken through Isaiah the prophet: "HE HIMSELF TOOK OUR INFIRMITIES AND CARRIED AWAY OUR DISEASES.""

Romans 8:11 NASB "¹¹ But if the Spirit of Him who raised Jesus from the dead dwells in you, He who raised Christ Jesus from the dead will also give life to your mortal bodies through His Spirit who dwells in you."

Mathew 15:30 AMPC "³⁰ And a great multitude came to Him, bringing with them the lame, the **maimed**, the blind, the dumb, and many others, and they put them down at His feet; and He cured them,"

I Peter 2:24 NASB "²⁴ …for by His wounds you were healed."

III John 1:2 NASB "² Beloved, I pray that in all respects you may prosper and be in good health, just as your soul prospers."

Being in good health and free from every kind of illness or disease is wonderful. Jesus healed us 2000 years ago. Jesus healed everyone that came to him for healing, and except for one occasion, they were all healed immediately. That one man had to go and wash in a certain pool. Like it said in

I Peter 2:24 "²⁴ for by his wounds you **were** healed." "Were" past tense, which means it has already been done for us. All that is required is to believe and trust Him to fulfill His word to you.

My wife had some lumps in her breast. We prayed, and when I took her to the hospital for a biopsy, she did not even take a suitcase. We both knew in our heart that she was healed. The doctors did a sonogram prior to her admittance, and found nothing. Jesus healed her. My wife's sister had a large tumor in her stomach area, we prayed, and the tumor disappeared. Another example is when I hurt my back, and could not straighten up or walk because of the pain. I prayed and the pain was gone, and I was able to straighten up and go to work that day.

Another example is you go to the doctor, and he says that you have the flu, or maybe cancer, or something that does not come in line with God's word. Who will you agree with? God or the doctor.

John 8:17 NASB "¹⁷ Even in your law it has been written that the testimony of two men is true."

Do not agree with the doctor, or repeat what he has said. What the doctor said may be true, but God said that you were healed. Believe it. That is who I am going to agree with every time. Now the doctor may have made a statement of fact, but according to God, it is not a statement of truth. God said that I was healed. That is what I will meditate on and believe. If your faith is not at that level yet, then I suggest that you take the medication he gives you, and believe and confess that you were healed in the name of Jesus.

12. We are full of wisdom and understanding

Wisdom and understanding are gifts from God. We are to seek wisdom, and gain understanding. Wisdom will help us in all of our everyday decisions.

Proverbs 3:13-22 NASB "¹³ How blessed is the man who finds wisdom And the man who gains understanding. ¹⁴ For her profit is better than the profit of silver And her gain better than fine gold. ¹⁵ She is more precious than jewels; And nothing you desire compares with her. ¹⁶ Long life is in her right hand; In her left hand are riches and honor. ¹⁷ Her ways are pleasant ways, And all her paths are peace. ¹⁸ She is a tree of life to those who take hold of her, And happy are all who hold her fast. ¹⁹ The LORD by wisdom founded the earth, By understanding He established the heavens. ²⁰ By His knowledge the deeps were broken up And the skies drip with dew. ²¹ My son, let them not vanish from your sight; Keep sound wisdom and discretion, ²² So they will be life to your soul And adornment to your neck."

Proverbs 8:17-21 NASB (Wisdom says) "¹⁷ I love those who love me, and those who seek me find me. ¹⁸ With me are riches and honor, enduring wealth, and prosperity. ¹⁹ My fruit is better than fine gold; what I yield surpasses choice silver. ²⁰ I walk in the way of righteousness, along the paths of justice, ²¹ bestowing a rich inheritance on those who love me and making their treasuries full."

One of the Apostle Paul's prayers that is found in the book of Ephesians. I pray this pray on a regular basis.

Ephesians 1:17-23 NASB "¹⁷ that the God of our Lord Jesus Christ, the Father of glory, may give to you a spirit of wisdom and of revelation in the knowledge of Him. ¹⁸ *I pray that* the eyes of your heart may be enlightened, so that you will know what is the hope of His calling, what are the riches of the glory of His inheritance in the saints, ¹⁹ and what is the surpassing greatness of His power toward us who believe. *These are* in accordance with the working of the strength of His might ²⁰ which He brought about in Christ, when He raised Him from the dead and seated Him at His right hand in the heavenly *places*, ²¹ far above all rule and authority and power and dominion, and every name that is named, not only in this age but also in the one to come. ²² And He put all things in subjection under His feet, and gave Him as head over all things to the church, ²³ which is His body, the fullness of Him who fills all in all."

James 1:5 NASB "⁵ But if any of you lacks wisdom, let him ask of God, who gives to all generously and without reproach, and it will be given to him."

I truly seek after wisdom, and ask every day for wisdom to guide me through the day. I have made it a habit to read as a prayer Ephesians 1:17-23 several times a week. None of us can hope to do Gods will and hear His voice without wisdom. God's word not only gives us answers and peace about every situation we face, but when you embrace and seek after wisdom, wisdom will bring you riches and honor as it said in Proverbs. God said so.

Wisdom will also be your guide, no matter what the circumstances. Through wisdom, God has directed me to various jobs when I worked contract. He also helped me to do my job when I had little understanding as to how to do my job. (I was hired to do one type of job, but given another type of job for which I had truly little knowledge.) On that particular job, I did not seek God's will to know if I should take the job, I thought it would be a great job, even though in my heart, I knew not to take the job. I was wrong, but in His wisdom, grace, and mercy, I was able to accomplish all that was required of me to complete the project.

13. We have great faith

We are given the same measure of Faith that Jesus, Peter, James, John, and Paul had. We are to use and develop that Faith to the point where we have no doubt that what we ask for will be given to us by the Father.

Mark 9:23 NASB "[23] And Jesus said to him, "If You can?' All things are possible to him who believes."

Mark 11:22-24 NASB "[22] And Jesus *answered saying to them, "Have faith in God. [23] Truly I say to you, whoever says to this mountain, 'Be taken up and cast into the sea,' and does not doubt in his heart, but believes that what he says is going to happen, it will be *granted* him. [24] Therefore I say to you, all things for which you pray and ask, believe that you have received them, and it will be *granted* him."

I urge you to read the bible out loud so you can hear His word spoken. It says in Romans that faith comes by hearing and hearing by the word of God. This is why I read out loud, so I can hear.

Romans 10:17 NASB "[17] So faith *comes* from hearing, and hearing by the word of God."

Hebrews 11:1 NASB "Now faith is the assurance of *things* hoped for, the conviction of things not seen. [2] For by it (faith) the men of old gained approval."

Hebrews 11:6 NASB "[6] And without faith it is impossible to please *Him*, for he who comes to God must believe that He is and *that* He is a rewarder of those who seek Him."

I John 5:4 NASB "[6] And without faith it is impossible to please *Him*, for he who comes to God must believe that He is and *that* He is a rewarder of those who seek Him."

Having faith, is the way God brings to you the things that you have ask for. He has laid up for you so much, it is hard to imagine, but we are not to be concerned how God will deliver His promises to us, only believe that He will. That is His job. For example,

Habakkuk 1:5 NASB says "[5] Look among the nations!

Observe! Be astonished! Wonder! Because *I am* doing something in your days— You would not believe if you were told."

Faith is the title deed to the things God has set aside for you. With faith, all things are possible to him who believes, and nothing will be impossible."

14. We are blessed and highly favored

Being blessed is a gift from God when we accept Jesus into our heart. All blessings come from our Heavenly Father. We as fathers desire that our children be blessed, and will try to give them the desires of their heart. God is now our Father, and desires that we have all that we need. He gives us favor with those around us. He changes rules and laws, so we can and will be promoted to a higher place. It is God's desire that you receive every Blessing He has for you.

Deuteronomy 28:1-6 NASB "[1] Now it shall be, if you diligently obey the LORD your God, being careful to do all His commandments which I command you today, the LORD your God will set you high above all the nations of the earth. [2] All these blessings will come upon you and overtake you if you obey the LORD your God: [3] "Blessed *shall* you *be* in the city, and blessed *shall* you *be* in the country." [4] "Blessed *shall be* the offspring of your body and the produce of your ground and the offspring of your beasts, the increase of your herd and the young of your flock." [5] "Blessed *shall be* your basket and your kneading bowl." [6] "Blessed *shall* you *be* when you come in, and blessed *shall* you *be* when you go out."

Psalm 21:1-6 NASB "¹ O Lord, in Your strength the king will be glad, And in Your salvation how greatly he will rejoice! ² You have given him his heart's desire, And You have not withheld the request of his lips. Selah. ³ For You meet him with the blessings of good things; You set a crown of fine gold on his head. ⁴ He asked life of You, You gave it to him, Length of days forever and ever. ⁵ His glory is great through Your salvation, Splendor, and majesty You place upon him. ⁶ For You make him most blessed forever; You make him joyful with gladness in Your presence."

Psalm 37:4-5 NASB "⁴ Delight yourself in the Lord; And He will give you the desires of your heart. ⁵ Commit your way to the Lord, Trust also in Him, and He will do it."

Luke 4:19 AMPC "¹⁹ To proclaim the accepted *and* acceptable year of the Lord [the day when salvation and the free favors of God profusely abound]."

Romans 5:15 AMPC "¹⁵ But God's free gift is not at all to be compared to the trespass [His grace is out of all proportion to the fall of man]. For if many died through one man's falling away (his lapse, his offense), much more profusely did God's grace and the free gift [that comes] through the undeserved favor of the one Man Jesus Christ abound *and* overflow to *and* for [the benefit of] many."

Romans 8:31-39 (MSG) "³¹⁻³⁹ So, what do you think? With God on our side like this, how can we lose? If God did not hesitate to put everything on the line for us, embracing our condition and exposing himself to the worst by sending his own Son, is there anything else he wouldn't gladly and freely do for us? And who would dare tangle with God by messing with one of God's chosen? Who would dare even to point a finger? The One who died for us—who was raised to life for us!—is in the presence of God at this very moment sticking up for us. Do you think anyone is going to be able to drive a wedge between us and Christ's love for us? There is no way! Not trouble, not hard times, not hatred, not hunger, not homelessness, not bullying threats, not backstabbing, not even the worst sins listed in Scripture: They kill us in cold blood because they hate you. We are sitting ducks; they pick us off one by one. None of this fazes us because Jesus loves us. I'm absolutely convinced that nothing—nothing living or dead, angelic or demonic, today or tomorrow, high or low, thinkable or unthinkable—absolutely *nothing* can get between us and God's love because of the way that Jesus our Master has embraced us."

Philippians 4:19 NASB "[19] And my God will supply all your needs according to His riches in glory in Christ Jesus. [20] Now to our God and Father *be* the glory forever and ever."

As you can see, we are blessed, and have the favor of God Almighty. He has given us everything so we could be with him in Heaven. Jesus paid the price for us so **we** could have the free gifs God wants us to have here on this earth. Most of God's gifts to us will not be needed when we get to Heaven. He wants us to live a life without any needs, to be blessed in every way.

Blessed, **favor**, and **grace** are all specific gifts from God. We have a desire to be blessed in everything that we do, and we want to have favor with everyone we come in contact with, and God's grace on our lives. But with God, He makes all things possible for us, and with His favor and His grace in our lives, there is nothing that can hold back the blessings freely given to us, except us. I was curious about what the dictionary had to say about favor, blessed, and grace. I used the Webster's 1828 dictionary because the definitions are based on the Bible.

Webster's 1828 dictionary defines **Favor** as "**1.** To regard with kindness; to support; to aid or have the disposition to aid, or to wish success to; to be propitious to; to countenance; to befriend; to encourage."

Webster's 1828 dictionary defines **Blessed** "*adjective* Happy; prosperous in worldly affairs; enjoying spiritual happiness and the favor of God; enjoying heavenly felicity."

Webster's 1828 dictionary defines **Grace** "**1.** Favor; good will; kindness; disposition to oblige another; as a grant made as an act of *grace* Or each, or all, may win a lady's *grace* **2.** Appropriately, the free unmerited love and favor of God, the spring and source of all the benefits men receive from him. And if by *grace* then it is no more of works. **Romans 11:5**. **3.** Favorable influence of God; divine influence or the influence of the spirit, in renewing the heart and restraining from sin. My *grace* is sufficient for thee.." **II Corinthians 12:9**

As you can see, God wants to Bless you and gives you Favor and Grace.

Mark 11:22-23 NASB "²² Have faith in God. ²³ Truly I say to you, whoever says to this mountain, 'Be taken up and cast into the sea,' and does not doubt in his heart, **but believes that what he says is going to happen, it will be *granted* him**."

God is giving you every advantage to be blessed. He is not asking you to do anything except to believe Him and what He is saying in His word.

I once had an evaluation of my performance at a job almost a decade ago. I prayed and asked that I have favor with my boss. I then received a 50% pay raise. My salary was doubled. Even though this has been many years ago, I pray each time I ask for a raise, I always expect a generous one. I will admit that some have been more generous than others, but a raise is always nice no matter how large or how small. It is a blessing and favor of God through His grace.

15. Angels watch over us

We have a multitude of angles watching over us. They are for our protection, and to do the bidding of God's words. I was driving on one of Houston's freeways. I almost never use the phone when driving. I had forgotten to call my wife, and as I was calling her, I looked down for just a second. In that second, I veered off the road at 65 mph and slammed into the dividing wall. instantly I saw a cloud surround me, and set me back on the freeway. I kept thanking God for His protection, and when I got to my destination and looked. I had absolutely no damage to my truck. I know the angels had helped me, and kept me safe.

Psalm 91:11-12 NASB "[11] For He will give His angels charge concerning you, To guard you in all your ways. [12] They will bear you up in their hands, That you do not strike your foot against a stone."

Psalm 103:20-21 NASB "[20] Bless the LORD, you His angels, Mighty in strength, who perform His word, Obeying the voice of His word! [21] Bless the LORD, all you His hosts, You who serve Him, doing His will."

Psalm 103:20 KJV "[20] Bless the Lord, ye his angels, that **excel in strength**, that do his commandments, hearkening unto the voice of his word."

Hebrews 1:14 NASB "[14] Are they not all **ministering spirits**, sent out to render service for the sake of those who will inherit salvation?"

Because you are a child of the Most High God, you have inherited His salvation, and the angels are working for you now. Put them to work on your behalf… God's angels are mighty. God has assigned angels to guard and watch over us. They are to carry out God's word. When you speak or pray the word of God, that will give them permission to act on your behalf. If you do not pray God's word, they are bound to not move on your behalf, but because you are now a child of God, the angels will work to bring to you what you have believed and asked for.

CHAPTER V

Have a Vision

CHAPTER V

Have a Vision

You should have a revelation of who's you are in Christ, and make a plan for your desires. Write your plans down. Ask God to give you the plan for your life if you do not have one. He said that he would give you the desires of your heart. Once you except Jesus into your heart, you belong to God, and He will give you, ideas, and a vision for your life. Get a vision of what you think God wants to do in your life. Talk to Him as if He were standing right next to you. He is, and wants to help you accomplish your dreams and goals. He put those desires in you, and He will show you how to accomplish those desires.

Job 8:9 NASB "[8] "But as for me, I would seek God, And I would place my cause before God; [9] Who does great and unsearchable things, Wonders without number."

Psalms 77:14 NASB "[14] You are the God who works wonders; You have made known Your strength among the peoples."

Proverbs 29:18 NASB "¹⁸ Where there is no vision, the people are unrestrained"

Habakkuk 2:2-3 NASB "² Then the LORD answered me and said, "Record the vision And inscribe *it* on tablets, That the one who reads it may run. ³ "For the vision is yet for the appointed time; It hastens toward the goal, and it will not fail. Though it tarries, wait for it; For it will certainly come, it will not delay."

Mathew 12:35 NASB "³⁵ The good man brings out of *his* good treasure what is good; and the evil man brings out of *his* evil treasure what is evil. ³⁶ But I tell you that every careless word that people speak, they shall give an accounting for it in the day of judgment. ³⁷ For by your words you will be justified, and by your words you will be condemned."

Next, sow a seed, and start thanking God for what he has showed you. Expect to receive it, and talk about it as though you already have it. You do have it in the spiritual realm. There is seed time, and harvest time. Once you plant the seed for your desires, it will grow and become your harvest. It is just like a farmer. One day he sows his seeds, he waits and watches it grow, then it is time for the harvest. The farmer plants just a few seeds compared to what is harvested.

Mathew 13:3-9 NLT "Listen! A farmer went out to plant some seeds. ⁴ As he scattered them across his field, some seeds fell on a footpath, and the birds came and ate them. ⁵ Other seeds fell on shallow soil with underlying rock. The seeds sprouted quickly because the soil was shallow. ⁶ But the plants soon wilted under the hot sun, and since they didn't have deep roots, they died. ⁷ Other seeds fell among thorns that grew up and choked out the tender plants. ⁸ Still other seeds fell on fertile soil, and they produced a crop that was thirty, sixty, and even a hundred times as much as had been planted! ⁹ Anyone with ears to hear should listen and understand."

After God has shown you what He wants you to do, Ask God how He wants you to proceed. Wait for it. Be patient, and above all, do not waver from your goal.

I John 5:15 NASB "¹⁵ And if we know that He hears us *in* whatever we ask, **we know that we have the requests which we have asked from Him**."

Mark 11:22-24 NASB "²² And Jesus answered saying to them, "Have faith in God. ²³ Truly I say to you, whoever says to this mountain, 'Be taken up and cast into the sea,' and does not doubt in his heart, but believes that what he says is going to happen, it will be *granted* him. ²⁴ Therefore I say to you, all things for which you pray and ask, believe that you have received them, **and they will be *granted* you.**"

Sow your seed. Take these scriptures and run with them. Meditate on them. Believe that they will bring your desires to pass. They are God's promises to you. He is faithful to fulfill your desires as you are faithful to Him. . Just have Faith that He is true to his Word.

There is a place in the back of this book to write down your vision and your desires.

CHAPTER VI

Conclusion

CHAPTER VI

Conclusion

You have so much power and authority in you through Jesus Christ our Lord. Words were used by God to create rather than to communicate, and we were created in His image and likeness. We are to choose our words carefully.

Mathew 11:20 NASB states "[20]...if you have faith the size of a mustard seed, you will **say** to this mountain, 'Move from here to there,' and it will move; and nothing will be impossible to you."

If the Bible says that I am forgiven, then I find scriptures that tell me I have been forgiven. If the Bible says that I am healed, then I find scriptures that tell me that Jesus has healed me. If the Bible says I am rich, I find the scriptures that say I am rich. I use words as Jesus did to restore, heal, provide, protect, and I expect Him to do the work.

I do not just read those scriptures one or two times but read them many times until it is in my heart, and I know that what I am saying is real because God said it about you and me. Whatever you are believing for God to give you, you have to Trust in God, as a little child, that he will give you the desires of your heart. Build your Faith by meditating on what God has said to you in His word.

Find the scriptures that pertain to your problem, or what you desire in your heart to have from God. Read them over and over until they are in your words when you talk to your friends or family, and you know in your heart that you have what God has been so gracious to give you.

Mark 11:22-24 NASB "²² And Jesus answered saying to them, "Have faith in God. ²³ Truly I say to you, whoever says to this mountain, 'Be taken up and cast into the sea,' and does not doubt in his heart, but believes that what he says is going to happen, it will be *granted* him. ²⁴ Therefore I say to you, all things for which you pray and ask, believe that you have received them, **and they will be *granted* you.**"

Mark 11:24 MSG "²²⁻²⁵ Jesus was matter-of-fact: "Embrace this God-life. Really embrace it, and nothing will be too much for you. This mountain, for instance: Just say, 'Go jump in the lake'—no shuffling or shillyshallying's—and it is as good as done. That is why I urge you to pray for absolutely everything, ranging from small to large. Include everything as you embrace this God-life, **and you'll get God's everything**.."

Mark 11:24 AMPC "²² And Jesus, replying, said to them, Have faith in God [constantly]. ²³ Truly I tell you, whoever says to this mountain, Be lifted up and thrown into the sea! and does not doubt at all in his heart but believes that what he says will take place, it will be done for him. ²⁴ For this reason I am telling you, whatever you ask for in prayer, believe (trust and be confident) that it is granted to you, **and you will [get it]**."

Mark 11:24 CEV " ²² Jesus told his disciples: Have faith in God! ²³ If you have faith in God and don't doubt, you can tell this mountain to get up and jump into the sea, and it will. ²⁴ **Everything you ask for in prayer will be yours if you only have faith**."

Mark 11:24 KJV "²³ For verily I say unto you, That whosoever shall say unto this mountain, Be thou removed, and be thou cast into the sea; and shall not doubt in his heart, but shall believe that those things which he saith shall come to pass; **he shall have whatsoever he saith**."

Mark 11:24 NLT "²² Then Jesus said to the disciples, "Have faith in God. ²³ I tell you the truth, you can say to this mountain, 'May you be lifted up and thrown into the sea,' and it will happen. But you must really believe it will happen and have no doubt in your heart. ²⁴ I tell you, you can pray for anything, **and if you believe that you've received it, it will be yours**."

It does not matter what version of God's word you feel comfortable with or have; God is wanting to bless you with his grace, mercy, and the power (authority) that is in His word. God does not ask you to pay for anything. He gave to us salvation; all we have to do is simply ask Him for it and believe in his son Jesus. God gave to us health and healing; all we have to do is simply ask Him for it. There is nothing that God will ever ask you to pay for. He does not ask you to work for it. Jesus paid the full price for everything when He went to the cross and died for us. All God has asked us to do is simply believe that he is true to his word, and have faith that he is true to His word.

Romans 3:4 NASB "⁴ May it never be! Rather, let God be found true, though **every man** *be found* **a liar**, **a**s it is written, "That You may be justified in Your words, And prevail when You **a**re judged."

As you can see, some scriptures can be used for more than one of God's promises that are our desires. Just as I have used various translations, find, and use various translations until you find what God says about you or to you, and you have a full understanding of what God is saying. God is giving you every advantage to be blessed. He is not asking you to do anything except to believe Him, and what He is saying in His word. Expect to see the move of God in every area of your life, and expect to see a change in your heart.

I have given you a lot of scriptures, but have just scratched the surface of what is in God's word for you. Some of the things that I have discussed you may not understand right now. Meditate on the scriptures, and God will show you and help you to understand His word through His Spirit. Find, read, meditate, and study them as often as you can. Add to the scriptures I have given to you. It will build your faith, and by exercising your faith, your faith will grow. It is so easy to follow what Jesus did as our example. He set, and was the example for all of us. He believed in God's word, He believed that God cannot and will not lie, and Jesus believes in you, and that you can have what you say according to God's Word. By using wisdom, you will not fail or fall into one of satan's traps of the mind, but win and overcome every obstacle or hinderance through the Word of God. He is your strength, and longs to give you His blessings, favor, and grace.

Here is another chance to make Jesus Christ the Lord of your life, it is a free gift from God. Simply pray, "Father, I believe that Jesus died for me and rose again. He took all my sins upon himself, and I ask that you forgive me and make me a new creature. Come into my heart".

If you have prayed this prayer, "Welcome" to the family of God. If you have no one to stand and agree with you when you pray, I will stand in agreement with you as you pray and ask God to come into your heart, and receive the desires of your heart.

Mathew 18:19-20 NASB "[19] Again I say to you, that if two of you agree on earth about anything that they may ask, it shall be done for them by My Father who is in heaven. [20] For where two or three have gathered together in My name, I am there in their midst."

If you have no one to stand in agreement with you, I will stand in agreement with you when you pray.

About the Author

Bill Larremore was born in what is called the heart of Texas, and raised in Brady then San Angelo, Texas. After high school, he spent a semester at Angelo State, then went into the U.S. Navy for just over 5 years. Bill's duty stations in Vietnam were the USS Outagamie County (LST-1073) and the USS Coral Sea (CVA-63). After 20 months at NAS Kingsville where his oldest daughter was born, Bill was honorably discharged from the U.S. Navy at NAS Kingsville (Kingsville, Texas).

Bill has always worked hard. It didn't matter what type of job he was doing. He has done a variety of jobs such as picking carrots for $.02 a bushel, building bard wire fences, and as a rod buster helper on a dam project in Robert Lee, Texas. After his years in the U.S. Navy, he spent 23 years as an industrial electrician, then 25 years as an electrical designer in the heavy industrial complex. During this time, he came to realize that words are especially important. Words get things done, and will keep a person safe. Words can bring happiness or grief. They can also be used to start wars or bring peace. Words also bring health, wealth, and wisdom. During the last 30 years, he started to really read and meditate God's word, and came to realize that the words that God used were to create. Having meditated on what God said, and how He said it. By excepting him as his savior, and having come to understood that our words have the same authority that God's words have. He has given that authority to all of us.

Your Vision - Desires

NOTES

NOTES

www.ingramcontent.com/pod-product-compliance
Lightning Source LLC
Chambersburg PA
CBHW072019290426
44109CB00018B/2285